# THE SMART KID'S GUIDE TO
# Moving

BY CHRISTINE PETERSEN • ILLUSTRATED BY RONNIE ROONEY

Published by The Child's World®
1980 Lookout Drive • Mankato, MN 56003-1705
800-599-READ • www.childsworld.com

Acknowledgments
The Child's World®: Mary Berendes, Publishing Director
Content Adviser: Philip C. Rodkin, Professor of Child
Development, Departments of Educational Psychology and
Psychology, University of Illinois
The Design Lab: Design
Red Line Editorial: Editorial Direction
Amnet: Production

Photographs ©: Shutterstock Images, cover, 1, 6, 7, 9, 10,
13, 15, 17, 21, 24, 25, 27, 28; iStock/Thinkstock, 5;
Thinkstock, 11, 18, 20, 29; Darren Baker/Shutterstock Images,
12; Suzanne Tucker/Shutterstock Images, 16; Olga Lutina/
Shutterstock Images, 19; ND Johnston/Shutterstock Images, 23;
Tatyana Vyc/Shutterstock Images, 26

ISBN 9781626873452
LCCN 2014930685

Printed in the United States of America
Mankato, MN
July, 2014
PA02224

## ABOUT THE AUTHOR

*Before becoming a freelance writer, Christine Petersen enjoyed diverse careers as a biologist and middle school science teacher. She has published more than 50 books for young people, covering topics in science, social studies, and health. Christine is a member of the Society of Children's Book Writers and Illustrators.*

## ABOUT THE ILLUSTRATOR

*Ronnie Rooney took art classes constantly as a child. She was always drawing and painting at her mom's kitchen table. She got her BFA in painting from the University of Massachusetts at Amherst and her MFA in illustration from the Savannah College of Art and Design in Savannah, Georgia. Ronnie lives on a U.S. Army base with her infantryman husband and two small children. Ronnie hopes to pass on her love of art and sports to her kids.*

# CONTENTS

# CHAPTER 1

# On the Move

Is your family is planning to move? You are not alone. Millions of Americans move every year. Throughout the nation's history, Americans have moved in search of a better life.

Many Native American tribes on the Great Plains used to be **nomadic**. They moved from place to place in different seasons. Everything the people needed could be packed up and moved. Moving was a lot of work. But it led them to new supplies of food and water.

For thousands of years, Native Americans were the only people living in the Americas. That changed when Spanish soldiers arrived in what is now Florida in the 1500s. Britain soon claimed land north of Florida. Its first colonies were Virginia and Massachusetts.

Over time, people came to the Americas from many different nations. Some moved here in search of riches or a better life. Others were brought as workers or slaves. The arrival of settlers changed life for Native Americans, too. Native Americans were forced to move and give up their land as settlers spread across the country.

*Some families move because they bought a new house.*

*Some people move to be closer to the rest of their family.*

Today people move for many different reasons. Their current home may be too small for a growing family. Or it may cost too much if a parent is sick or out of work. Some families move to live near friends and **relatives**. Others move because of a parent's new job. People may have to move suddenly after a **divorce** or death in the family. Sometimes, families have simpler reasons for moving. Maybe they hope to find a place with different weather or want to try life in a new city.

A move may take you just down the street or across town. It can lead your family to a new city or even to a different country! Those changes can seem scary at first. But it usually helps to stay positive. Think of the move as an adventure. You might not like everything about it. But you will probably find some nice surprises along the way.

Some people find that it helps to write or draw when life is changing quickly. You can write about your about feelings in a journal. Or you can try activities like this one: Make a list of your three favorite songs. Describe why you like each song. Now be happy! You can listen to music in your new home, too.

# CHAPTER 2

# Step by Step

There is much more to moving than taking your stuff from one place to another. Moving happens in stages. Taking part in every step of the move may help you feel more ready for it.

Moving usually begins when adults make a decision to change. They may include you in some of the choices that go along with moving, or they

*You might go house or apartment hunting with your family.*

may not. Maybe you will look at homes and schools together. Your family might take a trip to **explore** other neighborhoods or towns. If you cannot go in person, perhaps you can do an Internet search instead. (Ask an adult for help any time you go online!) It helps to learn about your new community before the move. You may discover parks, clubs, and activities that make the change exciting.

Saying good-bye is an important step before moving. Maybe you will throw a party to show

*Try to make a fun memory when you say good-bye.*

your friends you care. Or you might like to just do normal, fun things with them. This is a good time to give out cards with your new address and phone number. Do you have favorite teachers, coaches, or babysitters? Take a moment to write them thank-you notes. Places can be like friends, too. If you have time, visit the places you like best in your home and community. You can look forward to discovering new places very soon.

Moving can be a lot of work! Your family must pack up everything before a move. Friends and family sometimes come to help. Or your family might hire movers with a big truck. The boxes and furniture will be taken to your new home.

Unpacking is a separate stage of moving. You will probably unpack just a few things on your first night. It helps to have a few clothes, dishes, and bathroom supplies. Other things won't be put away for weeks. It can be tiring to live among boxes. Be patient. Before long, your family will find a place for everything.

*Offer to help carry boxes if you can!*

After you have moved, it is time to settle in. Your room is a good place to start. Ask your family members to help you put furniture where you like it. Take time to find the right places for your favorite clothes, toys, and books. Posters and photos will make your room feel more like home, too. Now you can get to know the neighborhood. Invite your family to go

Adults may not have as much time to spend with you during a move. They are busy with planning and packing. Ask if there are jobs you can do together. Maybe you can label boxes or fold clothes for packing. Work is always more fun when you can do it together.

*If your family says it's okay, do some decorating of your own.*
*Setting up your space will help you feel at home.*

for a walk or bike ride. Find the nearest movie theater, a fun restaurant, or a public swimming pool. You will enjoy these new places together as time goes by.

# CHAPTER 3

# Moving In

Moving brings up a lot of different feelings. You might feel sad or angry about leaving familiar places and friends. Perhaps you are a little scared about starting at a new school.

All those feelings are normal. Big changes are not easy for most people.

It can help to let your feelings out. Talk with family or other people you trust about the move. Together you can answer questions and solve problems. Look for the good changes that come with the move, too. Maybe you will have a bigger yard or bedroom. There might be a nice park nearby or new friends to share your interests with.

*Moving brings many changes to your life.*

*It might take a little while to get used to the noises in your new home.*

You have probably already thought about a few of the changes that come with moving. The first is leaving the apartment or house you are used to. The new place will look different. It will have unfamiliar sounds and smells. Those differences can be confusing at first.

It helps to spend time with your family. Lend a hand with unpacking. Your family will thank you, and you will learn where things are stored.

Explore the whole home as you settle in. You might find a cozy corner that is just right for reading. Maybe a certain window has the best view of the neighborhood.

Check out the exits in your new home with your family. Do you know what to do if there is an emergency? Practice a family fire drill. Practice what to do if the power goes out or there is a storm, too.

*Make sure you know where your family keeps flashlights in your new home.*

*Try saying "au revoir" instead of "good-bye."*
*That's French for "until we meet again!"*

After moving, you may not see familiar friends as often. Or you might never see them again. Your family members probably feel sad about leaving their friends, too. For many people, that is the most difficult change about moving. But a little planning can keep friends in your life. Make cards showing your new address and phone number. Include an e-mail address if you have one. You can give a copy of the card to each of your friends. Give them blank cards and ask nicely for their information in return. After the move, you can phone or write letters or e-mails.

Are you worried about losing touch with a parent or other family members after the move? You can write or phone them, too. Or use the Internet to make video calls. A memory book can also help you feel close to loved ones. Collect pictures of your friends and relatives for a memory book or bulletin board. You can keep it in your new room and see their faces any time.

*Keep photos of your friends and family to help you remember fun times together.*

*Your new school might seem really big, but you will learn your way around in time.*

You might have a lot of questions about going to a different school. "Will I fit in with the other kids? What will my teacher be like? How can I avoid getting lost?" Remember that you have started at a new school at least once before. Think back to your first year of preschool or kindergarten. You were much smaller then. But you made friends and found your way around the building. Now you are one of the bigger kids. You have so many skills! Use what you already know to make school easier. Start by simply saying hello to your new classmates and teachers. Ask to join a game at recess or sit with someone at lunch. It's okay if you don't meet a lot of people right away. Keep wearing your smile. It tells people you are ready to be a friend.

In a new place, you may meet kids who are interested in activities you have never tried. It can be good to try new things. But it's important to not change just so others will like you. Always stick to what feels right for you. A real friend won't ask you to do anything that is unsafe, unkind, or against the rules.

# CHAPTER 4

# An Easier Move

You might be excited to move. You might be nervous. Whatever your feelings, remember these tips that can make moving a little easier.

*Know where you are going.* Ask an adult to point out your new home on a map. Is it near your current home? Which roads will you take to get there?

How long is the drive on moving day? A map, the Internet, or an app can also help you learn more about your new community. Start by mapping a **route** between home and your new school. You can add other locations and routes as you get to know the neighborhood.

*If you're moving far away, use a country or world map to find your new home. If you're moving nearby, a city or state map should work.*

*Help pack your own things so you know what's in each box.*

*Be prepared.* Most of your stuff will be packed away for the move. How will you ever find it again? That's easy! Use a marker to write your name on every box that should go into your room. Even if you are very **organized**, moving day can be hectic! The boxes might be locked up in someone's car or a moving truck. You can prepare for this, too. Pack a special bag to carry with you. Put a pair of pajamas and a change of clothes inside. Include your toothbrush, toothpaste, and medicines. Don't forget your special stuffed animal or blanket. Is it a long drive to your new home? Pack a few favorite toys, books, and games so you won't get bored.

Your brothers or sisters may seem to fit in right away at school. Your parents might look perfectly happy in your new home. Don't worry if it takes you a while longer. Different people **adapt** differently to change. What matters most is that you keep trying.

*You can help out to make the move go smoothly.*

*Help out.* You can be a helper at every stage of your family's move. Think about some of the ideas in this book for helping before and after the move. On moving day, you can pitch in, too. Offer to sweep floors or dust after rooms are emptied. Check rooms and closets to make sure nothing is left behind. You can also look after younger brothers and sisters.

Do you have a pet? Make sure it does not escape as people go in and out.

*Stay in touch.* This tip has two meanings. It is important to stay in touch with friends and family in your old neighborhood. Send them letters and call whenever you can. But you must also **communicate** with the people you live with. Your parents want to know how you are doing after this big change. Tell them if you are worried or need help to solve a problem.

*Talk to your parents or another trusted adult if you are unhappy about the move.*

*Moving to a new community gives you a great
chance to try a new sport or activity.*

*Grow roots.* You did not just move into a new
home. You joined a new community. Making friends
at school is a good start. What about joining a
club or team? You can also meet people while doing
service that helps the community. All of these
activities help you put down roots. They make you
feel connected and strong.

A Roman teacher named Pliny the Elder thought about moving almost 2,000 years ago. As a young man, Pliny was a soldier. Roman soldiers traveled far and wide. Some spent years away from their families. It could be a lonely life. But Pliny learned something important during his time as a soldier. He wrote, "Home is where the heart is." What does that mean? Home is not a certain room, building, or town. It is a feeling of connection to others. You can carry that feeling wherever you go.

*Wherever you live, home is where your loved ones are.*

# TOP TEN THINGS TO KNOW

1. Each year, about one in every eight Americans moves.
2. Talk to others or write in a journal when you feel upset.
3. Moving is easier if you are organized.
4. Kids can be good helpers during a move!
5. It helps to learn about your new community before the move.
6. Pack a small bag to carry with you on moving day.
7. A map will help you find your way to important places in your new neighborhood.
8. Everyone adapts differently to change. It's okay if you need some time to get used to your new home and community.
9. You can stay in touch with old friends and family after the move.
10. Making friends and being active will help you feel like a part of your new community.

# GLOSSARY

**adapt** (uh-DAPT) To adapt is to get used to a change. It might take time to adapt after moving.

**communicate** (kuh-MYOO-ni-kate) To communicate is to share feelings and ideas. It's important to communicate with your family.

**divorce** (di-VORS) A divorce is the official ending of a marriage. Many people move after they get a divorce.

**explore** (ik-SPLOR) To explore is to travel and discover new things. Be sure to explore your new neighborhood.

**nomadic** (no-MAD-ik) People who are nomadic move from place to place in different seasons. Many Native American groups were nomadic.

**organized** (OR-guh-nized) Things that are organized are put together neatly or well planned. Try to stay organized during a move.

**relatives** (REL-uh-tivs) Relatives are family members. It is important to stay in touch with your relatives after you move.

**route** (ROOT) A route is a path for traveling from one place to another. Plan your route using a map.

## BOOKS

Deacon, Alexis. *A Place to Call Home*. Somerville, MA: Candlewick Press, 2011.

Murphy, Patricia J. *Moving*. Chicago: Heinemann Library, 2008.

Stones, Brenda. *Where We Live*. New York: Kingfisher, 2012.

## WEB SITES

Visit our Web site for links about moving: *childsworld.com/links*

Note to Parents, Teachers, and Librarians: We routinely verify our Web links to make sure they are safe and active sites. So encourage your readers to check them out!

## INDEX